The Habits That Define Us

Sandeep Poonian

Copyright © 2018 Sandeep Poonian
All rights reserved.

First Edition - 2018

Produced in association with Zenvizi Media Inc.

This paperback edition has been catalogued by the Published Herit-
age Branch, Library and Archives Canada
ISBN: 978-1-9995602-0-1

Cover art and design by Sandeep Poonian
Set in Garamond Pro

ABOUT THE AUTHOR

Sandeep Poonian has a degree in kinesiology.
He is a Canadian entrepreneur, philanthropist,
and now a published author. He currently
resides in the Vancouver area of British Columbia

For Joginder S. Poonian

June 4, 1933 – August 20, 2015

CONTENTS

Overture

"It is not the critic who counts; not the man who points out how the strong man stumbles, or where the doer of deeds could have done them better. The credit belongs to the man who is actually in the arena, whose face is marred by dust and sweat and blood; who strives valiantly; who errs, who comes short again and again, because there is no effort without error and shortcoming; but who does actually strive to do the deeds; who knows great enthusiasms, the great devotions; who spends himself in a worthy cause; who at the best knows in the end the triumph of high achievement, and who at the worst, if he fails, at least fails while daring greatly, so that his place shall never be with those cold and timid souls who neither know victory nor defeat."

-Theodore Roosevelt,

26th President of the United States of America

I have always wanted to write my own book. I can recall the first time I began to explore the idea of doing just that was around the time I had turned 9. That's quite a young age now that I think about it, however I was very fortunate when I was young to be able to use a personal computer. This was not something that either of my parents had grown up with, yet the opportunity to explore a whole new world through this unique device was incredible to say the least. And the computer that sat in my family room growing up, along with the Internet, opened my eyes to a whole new world outside of the small town I lived in. Although at that time what I was writing was not remotely sophisticated. I wanted to be the next J.K Rowling after reading the *Harry Potter* novels all summer long. In time I would find that writing my thoughts and finding a creative outlet for myself where my mind could run free had at many times provided me with the opportunity to simply understand just what was on my mind at the time. Fiction and storytelling had opened my eyes to the reality around me. During those years I would come up with numerous stories and creative ideas expressed through writing, cartooning, and so on. Looking back on it now, it was sheer childish wonder and creative madness. I had such artistic freedom and never felt bored by what I was learning. I would read books, play video games, and explore everything I possibly could by using that computer. However, I did not really publish any significant work for others to see. Well, besides an awful amount of gifs produced in my free time when I was younger, and the occasional piece of work my English teachers throughout high school believed were really outstanding. And now here I am. At 25, publishing my first book for others to read.

Following my 25th birthday, I came across a quote by boxing legend Muhammad Ali. If you are not familiar with Muhammad Ali and his work outside of the ring, I highly suggest you do some research for yourself. Ali has been a hero of mine for the longest time, and it would just not do his legacy any justice for me to begin to re-count all of his battles in and outside of the ring in this book. However this one quote did have a profound impact on me. Funny enough, this quote directly comes from a 1975 issue of *Playboy* Magazine. In the November 1975 issue Ali is quoted as saying that a man who views the world at 50, the same as he did when he was 20, has wasted 30 years of his life. He spoke these words while at a news conference in London, England and when he was asked about his philosophy on life. It is not the most elaborate or thought-provoking quote out there. And it's certainly not that philosophical. But it was simple, and it spoke to me and it made me think. You see, when I began to reflect on my own life, I began to see how much my views alone had changed from when I was 15. Or from when I was 20.

For several years of my early adult life, I was stuck in this position of internal chaos. I am not talking about chaos where I was in a state of physical or mental turmoil. Or in a state where my own reality was crashing around me. Chaos and it's opposition, Order, are two subjects that I will talk about further in this book.... The chaos that surrounded me was the incredibly competitive, and fast paced environment that I was in. At 18 I was accepted into one of the most prestigious, and internationally recognized post-secondary institution's in Canada; The University of British Columbia. From the beginning I was tossed into an environment I was not familiar with. My faculty, Arts and Sciences, and program, Bachelors of Science in Biology, was a highly competitive area of focus. At 18 I was running from lecture to lecture. From lab to lab. I was in a new city, away from the family and friends I was accustomed to that provided me with the social and emotional support for much of my life. I faced external chaos from new friends, romantic interests, work, and so on. I faced internal chaos from shifts in mood, new perspectives, and navigating throughout life to better understand my purpose on this planet. Surprisingly, I was not alone in all of this. I soon began to understand that other student's like myself were under immense amounts of pressure. And they were in similar stages of chaos and order.

Eventually, I would transition between periods of

chaos and order all throughout my undergraduate career. I acquired new skills that helped me teeter on the precipice of balance between the two. And I acquired new knowledge in just a short period of time. It was a great experience to go through in just four years. But balance can be quite fickle to maintain in this ever-changing world. At 22, I left the University of British Columbia. I was now beginning to undergo newer changes in my life and a new period of chaos. In the months since I had left and returned to the home I grew up in, my grandfather had passed away. Now, my grandfather had played a very important role in my early life. And due to our attachment, this sudden loss affected me deeply. He was born in the state of Punjab, India prior to the partition between what would later become India and Pakistan. He was among a handful of men that migrated to England in the late 1950's and early 1960's for job opportunities. He raised three of his own children, at times split between continents. And finally, my grandfather and my family had found their way to Canada. It was quite remarkable what he had done with the little resources that he had when compared to the abundance of resources that I grew up with. Whether it was fate, or pure determination that aided him along the way, he had lived a long and fruitful life. I credit my early discipline and attentiveness to him. He had guided me as a teacher and encouraged me greatly while I went through my early school years all the way until his passing.

At this point in time, while dealing with the loss, I was dealing with a new business that I was operating, financial situations, and a number of personal relationships. So to put it simply, there was a great deal of stress, depression, exhaustion, and pressure that I was under. This was another situation that I just was not prepared for. I had navigated my way through uncharted seas for four years, only to find myself shipwrecked on a island. However, just like I had previously done, I went through each of these situations and developed a better understanding of myself and my position within this world. I focused inward and began to understand the power of certain habits, how they can help balance the scale between Order and Chaos within our lives and maintain an overall balance that is required to live a healthy and fulfilling life. What I discovered for myself and the conclusions that I have developed as of this moment have had a profound impact on my life.

This book that you are about to read is a product 25 years in the making. It stems from my own experiences, and blatantly, from a sense of urgency when a quarter-life crisis begins to set in. This, I found, has been therapeutic in helping me deal with my own existentialism. To note however, *The Habit's That Define Us* is not an autobiography of my own life. It is not a self-help book that will give you all the answers that you need to live a productive and successful life. That is knowledge that is as elusive as the fountain of youth or the Philosopher's stone sought after many early chemists. And if a writer or any individual should try to sell you any product that will do that... Well, I certainly hope you will be skeptical. Throughout this book I will make no attempt to change your life. I will only give you the key's that may help you improve it. You are the captain of your own ship as you navigate it throughout the ever-changing current's that are life itself. In this book I will present to you areas of our lives where we must foster habits that I believe are crucial to live a life of balance between Order and Chaos. By the blessings and grace of Akaal Purakh (the Timeless One), I now present to you *The Habit's That Define Us*.

Chapter 1

The Mental

*"The person who has conquered their mind,
has conquered the world"*

-Guru Nanak Dev Ji
First Guru of the Sikh Religion

There is something intriguing about the human brain. As a physical structure it is the command center for all of the actions that take place consciously and unconsciously via the nervous system. In the area of performance based psychology there has been a great deal of focus behind how the mind can be "hacked" or used in order to increase performance. You may have heard of sayings such as "mind over matter" or "if you can dream it you can achieve it." Indeed, there has been a great deal of research and study into how mental processes contribute to increased productivity and performance. While there is enough compelling evidence that mental and therapeutic exercises can help increase mental performance, I am wary however to how some publications and public figures, such as motivational speakers, use the idea of mental processes in a very novel fashion. An example of this is the notion that by simple willpower one can overcome mental illnesses such as major depressive disorder or generalized anxiety disorder. This is a common theme that I have unfortunately come across in many self-help books. It is similar to telling someone to just be happy or to be positive. It does little to truly help the individual. When I was researching what habits we should foster each day to live a fulfilled and content life I considered the influence that they have on our mental processes. It is my belief that we should not only make an attempt to understand the physical aspects that make us human, but also our mental processes. So, it is my hope that you may also have a better understanding of the human psyche, from the mind to consciousness, through various perspectives.

So then what exactly is the human psyche? Or rather, what is human consciousness? This question has come up tirelessly in many different cultures and civilizations throughout human history. From scientists to philosophers, studying consciousness has lead to many different theories and assumptions of what it may be. Unfortunately, there is just not a single or simple answer for it. There are a number of approaches when it comes to answering this question. Take for instance in Greek mythology, it is said that the Titan Prometheus defied the gods by stealing the heavenly fire and giving it to humanity which in turn enabled the progress of civilization. Over time the interpretation of this story was that Prometheus had bestowed upon humanity a form of enlightenment, or higher consciousness through the gift of knowledge. This so called fire has also been used by other civilizations as well to explain an impactful gift that was bestowed upon humanity from the Gods. In each story there are certain repercussions that take place as a result of giving humanity this important tool. My interpretation of this is that it has been well understood for a very long time that the human mind is a considerable gift to humanity. It is what separates us from other species of animals that inhabit this planet. With that said however, it is a contentious topic that is still thoroughly being studied in modern academia.

The Psychological Approach

One attempt that we have then made is to study other parts of the mind in relation to consciousness. Understand, the field of modern psychology emerged in the 1800's and is composed of various schools of thought. Many psychologists since have attempted to explain the mind and our unique behaviors. This has of course led to areas of contention such as the nature versus nurture argument as to who we are as people and how we develop. Based on that argument there is the assumption that our behavior is either the result of pre-wiring and genetic inheritance, or a product of what we are exposed to as we age. Both streams of thought are certainly valid and there is considerable support for each side. So, to answer what the mind and consciousness is can be difficult due to the specific theories behind each.

" Just as treasures are uncovered from the earth, so virtue appears from good deeds, and wisdom appears from a pure and peaceful mind. To walk safely through the maze of human life, one needs the light of wisdom and the guidance of virtue."

-Siddharta Gautama,
The Buddha

One of the most common (and contentious) approaches to understanding the mind is the one proposed by Austrian neurologist Sigmund Freud. Freud determined that the mind and consciousness may exist outside of one another. He believed that what we deemed as the mind and consciousness may only occupy a small portion of our mental processes. Furthermore, Freud was also a strong believer that a person's past and childhood experiences determined their future behavior. Many of these experiences were also believed to originate from a place of sexual repression. For example, when a person experiences anxiety, it originates from traumatic experiences in an individual's past. These ideas formed what Freud deemed as psychoanalysis. Psychoanalysis was later further developed by Freud's colleagues and students. The premise of course being that by understanding the unconscious mind, therapeutic techniques and methods could be developed to help treat mental-health disorders. It was through his topographical model of the mind where he then described the features of the mind's structures and function. He split this model into different layers. On the surface there is consciousness which is composed of our thoughts based on what we focus on in the present. The second layer is what he describes as the preconscious, which is the information that we are able to recall from memory relatively easily. Finally, there is the layer of unconsciousness. This unconscious layer is where Freud determined most of our behaviors come from. It is the repository that makes us who we are based on our experiences. However, Freud's work was not short of controversy and is often criticized for being an incredibly narrow minded approach to the human psyche.

During the time that Freud's work was beginning to attract other scholars and individuals, Swiss psychiatrist and psychoanalyst Carl Jung added his own perspective to this theory. Jung agreed with Freud on the concept of the unconscious and added that the psyche is made up of several separate but interacting systems. These systems he determined were the ego, the personal unconscious, and the collective unconscious. According to Jung, ego represents the conscious mind through thought, memories, and emotions that a person is aware of. It is the ego that is responsible for our feeling of identity and continuity. Next, Jung interpreted the unconscious being represented by two separate factions. The personal unconscious contains the short-term information that may become repressed in memories over time. This includes our thoughts, feelings, attitudes, and memories on a single concept. When a number of these elements come together they form what are known as complexes. With more and more elements that become attached to the complex, there is a greater influence on the individual. As a result, our ego and personal unconsciousness can find themselves at odds. You may observe this when you experience moments of irritation, anger, or other reactionary emotions.

However, even Jung notes that the personal unconsciousness is superficial at best. This is where both Jung and Freud diverge the most through the notion of the collective unconscious.

Jung believed that the collective unconscious is a level of unconsciousness that is shared with other members of the human species. While controversial, he believed that this unconscious layer is composed of the latent memories of our ancestors and evolutionary past. He articulated that these ancestral memories and images that are imprinted into our very DNA are archetypes. An example of this is the fear of the dark, snakes and spiders, which has been observed in cultures around the world. Jung believed that our primitive past is what forms the basis for the human psyche and directly influences our present behavior. He narrows down the archetype of the collective unconscious into four archetypes; the persona, anima/animus, shadow, and the self. The persona is the mask that we outwardly display to the world. The persona conceals our real self, like an actor playing a part. The anima/animus is the mirror image of our biological sex which manifests the attitudes and behaviors of the opposite sex. So, the psyche of a woman contains masculine aspects, and the psyche of a man contains feminine aspects. The shadow archetype is the more primitive aspect of our personality. It is the source of our creative and destructive forces. Finally, there is the self-archetype which Jung believes is what reflects the individual's own experiences. With these archetypes in mind Jung believes this is what the basis of the human psyche is.

Another important figure to discuss during this time is a contributor of the psychoanalytic movement; Alfred Adler. Adler was a physician, psychotherapist, and founder of Adlerian Psychology. Like Freud and Jung, Adler developed his own approach that can almost be considered the basis for modern cognitive behavior therapy. I say almost because much of the foundational concepts behind Adler's theories are similar to those proposed by Albert Ellis and Aaron Beck which are now considered cognitive therapy. His divergence of sorts from Freud's ideas placed the importance on the individual and how the conscious process of the mind shapes our personalities, behavior, and general fate. He examined what drives us, such as the forces underlying our motivations as individuals. Adler believed that this force that propelled us in such a manner cognitively was the desire to strive for perfection. While Freud had focused on the past being the cause for many problems an individual may face, Adler was more forward looking. To Adler, his motivation force was about an individual moving toward the future. This concept where we are drawn towards our goals, purposes, and ideals is known as teleology. To put it simply, we as individuals are not living life in a cause and effect manner. That means that as individuals we have a choice, and our own realities can change along the way as we pursue our ideals. The past does not determine our future. We are not headed in a direction based on predetermination. At least that's how Adler puts it.

While Adler had proposed his theory of Teleology, a question began to perplex him. If humans are pulled towards perfection, finding fulfillment, and reaching self-actualization, then why does a large population still end up feeling unfulfilled and far from perfect? There must still be a reason for why some individuals are not able to realize their true selves and ideals. This, he determined, was due to a sense of inferiority that grows larger as we age. When an individual fails, and is not able to fall back in place, they may get discouraged and retreat inwards. Think about it like this. As a child you may have had certain hobbies and activities that you liked to explore. In this case, I am going to choose the sport of basketball. Now there may be a time when you were playing basketball and you made a lot of mistakes. You may have tripped over your own feet during a game, much to the embarrassment of your parents or others in your immediate social circle. Now, the sport that was originally an interest to you, makes you feel discouraged. This carries on as you try to avoid the sport during gym class in middle and high school. You begin to attribute this to other parts of your life. Maybe this is why you are overweight? Maybe sports are just not for you? Do you see where I am going with this?

As we age, this inferiority complex grows and seeds a doubt that fosters a neurosis that develops. An individual may become more insecure, indecisive, cowardly, withdrawn, and so forth. When the individual reaches such a state, they may feel a sense of uneasiness and develop passive-aggressive and manipulative traits. They seek validation from others around them and affirmations that give a false sense of superiority. Now, not everyone goes through this, and some do not develop passive-aggressive or manipulative traits. They may develop other personality traits as a result. Some individuals may even develop a superiority complex, where they cover their own insecurities by pretending to be superior. This leads to your average playground bully or vindictive and controlling individual. As you can see, there is great deviation from the unconscious in the case of Adlerian psychology. Therefore, when we try to understand the "mental" process behind what makes us who we are, there are considerable factors to examine.

"Never lose your self-respect, nor be too familiar with yourself when you are alone. Let your integrity itself be your own standard of rectitude, and be more indebted to the severity of your own judgement of yourself than to all external precepts. Desist from unseemly conduct, rather out of respect for your own virtue than for the strictures of external authority. Come to hold yourself in awe, and you will have no need for Seneca's imaginary tutor."

-Baltasar Gracian

Understanding Motivation

I often find when I work with my colleagues or enjoy a conversation with friends there comes a time when someone mentions how demotivated they are feeling.

"I want to go to the gym but I just do not have the motivation to go…"

For some reason or another we turn to motivation and consider it to be the reason why we are not able to accomplish our tasks. From reading the previous section you may have come to understand that that is hardly what is taking place. Motivation is a very complex process that is best understood when we break it down. It is the reason for our actions, desires, and needs. Current conventional thinking is that our motivations can be divided into intrinsic and extrinsic factors, or be represented by a desire to satisfy human needs.

Intrinsic motivation is noted as being the behavior that is driven by internal rewards. When we feel motivated without the intention of obtaining a reward external to us we are acting from a place of intrinsic motivation. For someone to truly develop intrinsic motivation, they first must have a relatively high degree of self-determination and an increase in perceived competence. This is a very important point to pay attention to because this is the motivation that people often feel they are lacking in. The opposite of this is extrinsic motivation which occurs out of desire to obtain a reward outside of the individual. An example of this is competition which encourages the performer to win and beat others. This of course often comes from a place of very little intrinsic reward to the person who is competing.

There are additional competing theories behind what drives us as human beings. One of these theories is Abraham Maslow's hierarchy of needs. Like Adler, Maslow determined that self-actualization is the goal that all individuals are striving for. He believed that humans are inherently good and that they possess a constantly growing inner drive. Furthermore, Maslow believed that our state of motivations can be determined by a set of hierarchic needs. Our very motivations, he believed, come from our needs not being satisfied. From the most basic needs to the most complex he believed these classes needed to be satisfied:

- Physiology
- Safety and Security
- Social Relationships
- Self esteem
- Self-actualization

Since the early 1970's another theory was proposed to understand motivation. Self-determination theory, as it would come to be known, examines how an individual's behavior reflects their self-motivation and self-determination. Self-determination theory identifies that when a set of needs are satisfied this will lead to an increase in performance and allow for optimal function and growth. The needs that must be satisfied include competence, relatedness, and autonomy. These three psychological needs are believed to motivate the individual, and when they are not allowed to flourish, the individual's motivations, productivity and general happiness decrease. Therefore, it is important that the individual develops a need to master their inner forces (competency), develop a set of skills (relatedness), and build their own internal self-confidence (autonomy).

Keys to understanding the Mental

We are all unique individuals that observe the world around us through contrasting perspectives and lenses. Each of our experiences and behaviors can best be related to our overall psyche. The complexity of the human brain and the mental processes that make us who we are should not be discounted, especially when we are trying to live a fulfilling and balanced life. However, I do not believe that we should discount how very similar we are as well in spite of our individuality. It is because we are very similar to one another on a cognitive level that we can use intervention techniques to improve our mental health and wellbeing. If you are struggling mentally then I encourage you to seek help. Whether it be through cognitive-behavioral therapy or other avenues. It is naïve to think that you can fix a problem in your life by simply wishing it to be fixed. You must take action. In the same way that you would not apply a small bandage to a deep wound to stop the bleeding, you cannot patch up what is happening between your ears so easily.

This section that I have written is meant to serve as a stepping stone for you to understand a little bit more about how you can use the habits that I list later in this book to their full advantage. I have only scratched the surface in this chapter and I encourage you to educate yourself further on the human psyche and the brain.

Chapter 2

The Physical

"It's like chopping down a huge tree of immense girth. You won't accomplish it with one swing of your axe. If you keep chopping away at it, though, and do not let up, eventually, whether it wants to or not, it will suddenly topple down. When that time comes, you could round up everyone you could find and pay them to hold the tree up, but they wouldn't be able to do it. It would still come crashing to the ground... But if the woodcutter stopped after one or two strokes of his axe to ask the third son of Mr. Chang, 'Why doesn't this tree fall?' And after three or four more strokes stopped again to ask the fourth son of Mr. Li, 'Why doesn't this tree fall?' he would never succeed in felling the tree. It is no different for someone practicing the Way."

-Zen Master Hakuin

Environment

You are the product of millions of years of evolution. Let that sink in for a moment. The first ancestors of modern humans are believed to have walked the Earth five to seven million years ago. These primitive ancestors of ours were able to successfully survive and reproduce overtime so much so that humanity has currently stretched to all four corners of the globe. Millions of years ago, these early ancestors did not have sharp claws to defend themselves from predators and stood at less than five feet tall. They were not able to run at top speeds like the cats that lived in the open savanna. They were, in simple terms, at a huge disadvantage. It is a miracle that a group of early humans was able to survive at all under these conditions without going extinct. While trees may have given monkeys and other apes salvation, the East African ground was hardly a source of comfort. It is truly remarkable to think that our primitive ancestors were able to navigate the harsh environments and climate of East Africa, full of predators with fangs and other poisonous species. And they accomplished this all without modern medicine, sophisticated technology, or the Internet.

In a relatively short period of time (in terms of evolution), these feeble humans were able to advance in the animal kingdom as fierce hunters. So how did this happen? There are currently many theories that help explain this question. For one thing, these early humans had developed the ability to walk upright, which is termed as bipedalism. Studies have indicated that this may have occurred over time in order to free up the hands for tasks such as grasping, reaching, and carrying objects. In turn this would help save energy during locomotion, enabled the ability to run for long distances, and provide an enhanced field of vision. With regards to that last point, there is a significant advantage that visual acuity played in survival. Over time a large number of anatomical changes took place. However, for all the positive changes that occurred as a result of bipedalism, there were certain drawbacks. Bipedalism resulted in a shortening of the pelvis and smaller birth canals. And in addition to that, growth of the brain and skull posed a problem. These changes then made it increasingly difficult to bear children.

As I just mentioned, a rather large evolutionary change that occurred over time was the growth of the human skull (encephalization). In comparison to other primates, the human brain continues to increase in size during postnatal brain growth. However, the most important fact to understand here is that brain size does not equal higher levels of intelligence. What makes the human brain so unique in comparison to other species that inhabit this planet is the way it is structured. The human brain has increased temporal lobes, which contain areas for language processing, and a prefrontal cortex that has been related to complex decision-making and moderating of social behavior. So, although our early ancestors did not have the advantages of some predatory animals, they did possess a more developed brain. Quite possibly the most important biological traits that have come from the development of the brain include vision, socialization, and reasoning.

"If you put an empty gourd on the water and touch it, it will slip to one side. No matter how you try, it won't stay in one spot. The mind of someone who has reached the ultimate state does not stay with anything, even for a second. It is like an empty gourd on the water that is pushed around."

-Takuan Sōhō

Vision

The human eye, is simply a marvel when you consider its significant contributions. Through millions of years of evolution, the human eye has aided in the survival of our species. Like early humans that we've descended from and our primate relatives, our eyes are located in a full-frontal position on our face. This evolutionary advantage allows us to possess binocular and stereoscopic vision. Typically, many predatory organisms such as lions and owls possess this evolutionary trait. They, like us, have eyes that are considerably sensitive to light. For primates living in the treetops, having this kind of vision allowed them to navigate through their surroundings, to find food, and to avoid predators. Life in the treetops was fast paced, and if the eyes of early primates were not evolved to meet such demands, they would not be able to survive. For early humans that were living in the open lands of Africa, vision played another role. Open land exposed these early humans to more dangers than ever before. As a nomadic group of people, they moved from one area to another, but had to pay great attention to their surroundings. Unlike the safety that the treetops provided, the open land introduced the challenge of hunting prey for food and paying close attention to new environments. When standing upright they were able to observe large distances and identify predators. And the sensitivity to light allowed them to move in the night, especially in the presence of predators that they could observe. This led to greater attention and focus that was required for survival. When these humans focused on their surroundings they may have picked up on certain patterns of both predators and prey from foot print and signs, to how the terrain shifted in places. It may be possible that the need for increased attention to detail in our surrounding environment is what enabled humanity to progress and avoid dying out.

Unlike other animals that may scan their environment, humans are quite perceptual. Instead of seeing a just a tree, humans could focus in on each individual branch or leaf. Because of such a heightened level of focus, our primitive ancestors were also able to detach themselves from their surroundings and give greater attention to what was not only in front of them on a superficial level. Such intense focus allowed our early ancestors to notice patterns, anticipate scenarios, and make predictions that increased probability of survival. This high level of attention and focus has come to be known as the top-down and bottom-up strategy of information processing by the brain. Typically, sensory input is considered bottom-up, while higher cognitive processes are considered top-down.

Consider this. In our modern day we are exposed to a great deal of sensory information. From the text message you receive on your phone, to the movie playing on your television, a lot of this information floods our senses. However, with all of this sensory data coming in, an estimated 90% is lost. Therefore, much of what is processed is based on the reliance on past experiences to construct our perception of reality. It is plausible that this top-down approach is what allows us to screen out distractions and focus our mind on a single task or a series of complex patterns. The bottom-up approach is referred to being more primitive, forged by evolution, is impulsive, uncontrolled, and often stimulated by fear and other emotions. In comparison to other species of animals, humans may have developed the ability to utilize the top-down process to attentively focus in on the surroundings around them for survival. While the human brain can still be stimulated bottom-up, it is the top-down approach that enables us to observe the world around us with greater detail.

Understanding the Physical

It is incredibly naïve to believe that we can go against millions of years of evolution to change our lives. Instead, we should look to use these key evolutionary traits to our advantage. Humanity is truly blessed to have a brain with such plasticity that allows us to adapt to the environment that we are in. Like our early ancestors, we are constantly learning and developing. Therefore, when you venture on a path of self-growth you should not feel ashamed for wanting to improve or to better yourself. You do not owe it to anyone to be the same person that you were years, months or days ago. You do not even have to be the same person that you were fifteen minutes ago if it is in the pursuit of self improvement. It is instinctual to do so. It has been essential to our survival as a species on this planet. It is my hope that the areas of focus that I present to you later in this book can be used to your own advantage to help you develop proper lifelong habits that you can stick to.

Chapter 3

Order and Chaos

"We are living in a culture entirely hypnotized by the illusion of time, in which the so-called present moment is felt as nothing but an infinitesimal hairline between an all-powerfully causative past and an absorbingly important future. We have no present. Our consciousness is almost completely preoccupied with memory and expectation. We do not realize that there never was, is, nor will be any other experience than present experience. We are therefore out of touch with reality. We confuse the world as talked about, described, and measured with the world which actually is. We are sick with a fascination for the useful tools of names and numbers, of symbols, signs, conceptions and ideas."

-Alan Watts

Life is suffering. Buddhist's have contemplated the meaning of life for centuries. Man himself has contemplated his own existence for more than a millennia. The purpose of our life, our place within this universe, is still a contentious subject among people. The very thought influences our day to day tasks, religions, politics, and the nature of good and evil. And at the root of it all is the human life. We as humans, through the marvels of civilizations, science and technology, are imbued with such ego that we rationalize our very existence as something important. The fact of the matter is that we are not. Although we are living in perhaps the greatest time in human history, we are fallible organisms. Once we understand that we can begin to understand and perhaps even find our own purpose within life.

I once picked up a book by Viktor Frankl called *Man's Search for Meaning*. In the book, Frankl chronicles his own experiences as an Auschwitz concentration camp inmate during World War II. What intrigued me was how Frankl described life having meaning even under the grotesque conditions at Auschwitz. From his own experiences Frankl concludes that under all circumstances, even the most miserable ones, life has meaning. He goes on to further state that this meaning that we search for within our own lives can be found by 1) creating a work or doing a deed; 2) by experiencing something or encountering someone; and 3) by the attitude we take toward unavoidable suffering. Much of what Frankl was describing paralleled my own interpretations of life. Although my experiences were not similar to his, I was familiar with a few of his points through my own religion.

I can remember a time when I was under a great deal of stress. It was during my second year at UBC where I was enrolled in full time classes. Full time, as in I was enrolled in five lecture courses each with their own labs and a tutorial for both of my semesters over eight months. That's about eleven courses a semester. Six years later and I can still remember what my life was like back then. From Monday to Friday I would get up at 6am, grab some breakfast at one of the cafeterias on campus, and head off to my first lecture of the day at around 8:30am. Once the eighty minute lecture was over I would have about ten minutes to run over to the next building for a three hour lab. Sometimes these labs would take the full three hours or so, and on some fortunate days would end much earlier. I would then enjoy some lunch at a campus cafeteria again with some of my peers that were living the exact same lifestyle. Once lunch was over with, I would attend another lecture, hit the library or drag myself back to my dorm room. Sometimes it was for a nap and sometimes to actually study so that I did not fall behind in my studies. After dinner I would continue studying or go to another three hour lab in the evening until 9pm. Following that I had just about one hour to go to the gym on campus. And finally I would come back and hop into bed by 11 pm. This tiresome routine carried on, even when temperatures fell to -23 degrees Celsius in Kelowna. When the weekend would swing by I would find myself studying during the day, catching up on other social and personal responsibilities, and going out for the night with friends. By the time my winter semesters had finished I was completely burnt out. I can remember coming home for the summer break and hiding in my basement with the only comfort being video games and home cooked meals. And then I went back to school for six more weeks of condensed courses during a summer term. It was incredibly exhausting and left me in a position of discomfort.

What I had experienced in a year had left me completely drained, both mentally and physically. Walking into my second year of university I was close to 165 pounds. By the time my winter semester had ended I had weighed in at 141 pounds. That was not my intended goal. I made sure to consistently eat so that I would not neglect my body during this stressful time. I made it a priority to go to the gym four to five days a week. But even then I had lost weight. I hurt one of my hip flexor muscles while working out and saw a significant decrease in my performance at the gym. I did not sleep well. I was simply overworked, and too stubborn and perhaps even blinded by everything that was happening around me to do anything about it. Reflecting back on it now truly allows me to see how chaotic my life was during that time. What I soon discovered however was that I was not the only undergraduate student going through this chaos. A large number of students from all walks of life were struggling and trying to find their own order and the motivation to continue. Ironically, I had also met students that were managing very well to this lifestyle. But some of them were bored and uninterested in their education. It was as if these two samples of students were on exact polar ends of one another, with one end attracting students to complete chaos and other to complete order.

> *"In a position of utter desolation, when man cannot express himself in positive action, when his only achievement may consist in enduring his sufferings in the right way - an honorable way - in such a position man can, through loving contemplation of the image he carries of his beloved, achieve fulfillment."*

> *-Viktor E. Frankl*

The Basis of Order and Chaos

In Ancient Chinese philosophy there is the analogy of Yin and Yang. It is believed that both forces are complimentary, interconnected, and interdependent in the natural world. Each may give rise to each other and can be represented by tangible dualities. The common interpretation of yin and yang in western culture is that one represents good and the other represents bad. That interpretation is quite an oversimplification however. Rather, it is the duality of the two forces that become complimentary. It is from here that I began to explore the duality between order and disorder. Or rather, order and chaos.

Order and chaos can also be misinterpreted as each standing for good or bad. That is not the case and I would argue that both order and chaos can be viewed as the opposite and the same sides of a coin. My interpretation of order and chaos builds off of Friedrich Nietzsche's philosophy of embracing conflict and suffering throughout life. He argues that for one to have a fulfilling life, the difficult must be embraced. For what is life, full of happiness and bliss, if it is not met by despair and sadness? By his accounts, most of human achievement throughout history has come about from some degree of torment and pain. Would we have advanced in science and technology without the atrocities of the Second World War? Could humanity have prospered to this point in modern human history without devastating vast ecosystems through pollution and our obsessive need for malls and shopping centers? Perhaps. And perhaps we would not have made it this far without such a sacrifice. That is troubling and quite disturbing to think about. But that is the nature of things and the reality before us. At least that is interpretation the Nietzsche came up with between suffering and prosperity in life. My interpretation of this is that our lives are governed by the states of Order and Chaos. If we cannot find balance between the two, we may lose all sense of reality.

It is rather odd to consider but think about it for a minute. Life is suffering. Buddhist's believe that this suffering is due to attachments to objects of impermanence. To put it as simply as possible, we suffer when we dwell on things that do not last. This can be the cars we enjoy driving, the clothes we enjoy wearing, or the people that we enjoy keeping in our company. This eventually leads to suffering via dissatisfaction, conceit, and our inevitable ego once we do not have what we have always sought. There is also suffering in chasing these objects in the hopes of having it one day. Like money. Lots of money…. I agree with this interpretation of life being full of suffering. Like a hamster on a wheel we run in place constantly chasing something that will one day be of little to no value in the grand scheme of things. I also agree with Nietzsche's philosophy of suffering. But why must this duality take place between suffering and prosperity throughout life? Is it due to a higher power or intelligent design? Whatever the case may be, there is a great deal of argument that can take place to justify that life is suffering, or that it is not. But by my accounts, and my own personal interpretation based on the philosophies of others such as Siddhartha Gautama, the Buddha, Nietzsche, and even Guru Nanak of my own Sikh religion, life in all its highs and lows is due to the duality between Order and Chaos.

Order and Chaos is what birthed this universe into being, if you follow the principle of the Big Bang theory. The theory suggests that from a very high density and high temperature state the universe began to expand. From the immediate chaos that took place an eventual order was put into place. As the universe cooled, subatomic particles formed. And eventually, after 13.8 billion years this event took place, we have our current universe. On a cosmic scale however, chaos and order still exists. Just like the Yin and the Yang, Order and Chaos live in harmony with one another in a repetitive circle or as two scales of balance. This same chaos and order is what drives our very lives in the very plane that we humans exist in daily. There is both order and chaos when we are successful. And there is order and chaos when we are not. Try as hard as you might, you cannot have one without the other. That is precisely what Nietzsche articulated more than a hundred years ago. We are gifted order and chaos the moment we are birthed from our mothers and pushed out into this life. The only escape that we have from order and chaos is at the moment we die. And who even knows what happens when Death comes. That is even more order and chaos, but not for the one who is gone! This is life. This is your life, governed by Order and Chaos.

As you transition into the next section of the book you will now be more familiar with the concepts I talk about. Consider the biological properties that make us human. And consider the psychological properties that define us. Finally, it is my hope if you are reading this that you can come to understand the order and chaos in your own life… Make no mistake, one is not better than the other. Both are necessary to coexist in harmony for you to have any purpose or fulfillment in this life. When one side of this scale outweighs the other, we end up in a very lonely place. It is a purgatory of self-driven conceit. It is a point when we lose the reigns of our life and plummet headfirst off a cliff and lose all sense of reality. It is a point when we hopelessly steer our ship through the ever changing currents of life without any sense of direction. It is when we cannot find our purpose or define ourselves. It is a Hell in biblical terms. That is the Hell that you are in right now if you cannot find the balance between order and chaos.

Thunder and wind: the image of DURATION.

Thus the superior man stands firm
And does not change has direction. Thunder rolls, and the
wind blows; both are examples of extreme mobility and so are
seemingly the very opposite of duration, but the laws govern-
ing their appearance and subsidence, their coming and going,
endure. In the same way the independence of the superior
man is not based on rigidity and immobility of character. He
always keeps abreast of the time and changes with it. What
endures is the unswerving directive, the inner law of his be-
ing, which determines all his actions.

-The I Ching,

The Book of Changes, China 8ᵗʰ Century B.C.

Chapter 4

Make your bed

In the morning, when you
rise unwillingly,
let this thought be present:
"I am rising to the
work of a human being."

-Marcus Aurelius

In the past year I came across a YouTube video where a United States Admiral was addressing a graduating class. It was one of those videos that seemed to be in my recommendations side bar on the site. And, for all intents and purposes, I clicked on it to just pass some time. Maybe it would inspire me or help intrigue me somehow. Thankfully, it did. During his speech, Admiral William H. McRaven declared that the single task that you should set out to accomplish every day is to simply make your bed. He argued, that before jumping to change the world or to accomplish any big task, the simplest task that should be performed each day is to properly make your bed. Making your bed each day helps you develop the discipline in maintaining a routine. And at the end of the day, whether it was a productive or unproductive day, you would return home to a neatly made bed. For most people this is a simple concept to understand. But there is a little more to the making your bed analogy than you may think. If every single person were to get up in the morning and make their beds that would be wonderful, but it does not make you a highly successful or productive person necessarily. Regardless of whether you make your bed or not in the morning, the most important message here is about developing a sense of discipline and routine for the beginning of the day.

If you routinely sleep for up to eight hours a night, that's about one-third of your day devoted to rest. If you work a typical nine to five job, then that's another one-third of your day devoted to work. And so here you are, left with one-third of your day to devote to whatever you desire. In a more realistic situation, you may devote this time to social activities and other responsibilities. Maybe you have children you are responsible for taking care of. Perhaps you devote time to taking care of your own well-being, whether it be through physical exercise or moments of mental clarity. Regardless, for a majority of adults this becomes a routine. Not everyone on this planet has the same exact daily routine. That would be crazy. But as humans we all undergo a period of wakefulness and rest.... At least if we are healthy. We all wake up at some time and go about our day. And that's where the analogy of making your bed comes into play. What we do from the moment we wake up can impact how the rest of our day will go. It is for this reason that I believe that we must pay careful attention to our habits following wake-fulness.

Making your bed is easy. For myself I find that after I wake up I will go into my daily routine of reciting *Japji Sahib*, the morning prayer recited by followers of the Sikh religion. This is something that I have come close to routinely do for 20 years of my life. Much of this I learned from my grandfather. I can recall from my earliest memories that my grandfather would wake up every morning at 5am, have a morning shower, and recite *Japji Sahib*.

Truth be told, I would only get up at 5am every now and then to have an excuse to watch repeats of my favorite show, *Dragon Ball Z*, on tv. Within the past few years however I began to notice how much of an impact that waking early in the morning and starting the day off with my prayers had on the rest of my day. This was my order. On occasion I would wake up at a late time, passed 8am for me, and forego my prayers and other early morning routines. I might even skip breakfast entirely and not give myself room to plan ahead. The rest of the day I would either be irritable, unfocused, and often lazy. This was my chaos. When there was a greater pull to one side or another, it would become difficult for me to go about my days as I would hope for it to. I'm not suggesting that you should wake up at the same time every morning, recite your prayers, and be out the door ready to tackle the day like some clockwork robot. And I am definitely not suggesting that you should wake up at whatever time you wish, forego all responsibilities and neglect your personal hygiene. But you should develop or find a routine that you can stick to from the moment you wake up. When you do that, it will not be as overly difficult for you to prepare for the day ahead of you. And if you fall along the way, such as missing your third alarm or even spilling your breakfast, you will be okay. That is simply life, and you will find that you can teeter on the order and chaos of your mornings in a much more balanced fashion.

"Making my bed correctly was not going to be an opportunity for praise. It was expected of me. It was my first task of the day, and doing it right was important. It demonstrated my discipline. It showed my attention to detail, and at the end of the day it would be a reminder that I had done something well, something to be proud of, no matter how small the task."

-William H. McRaven, *Make Your Bed: Little Things That Can Change Your Life... And Maybe the World*

Keys to starting your day

My approach to developing the morning habits necessary to start a productive day are quite simple. As previously mentioned, I examined the routines that I grew up with. I already had a strong foundation that was built over many years of following the same routine for starting my day. What was required was the routine prior to rest and adjusting what I did from the moment I woke up. I made this very personal for myself. Before bed I began to make it a habit of putting my phone away on my bedside table or on a dresser. I would change the settings to leave it on the general "Do Not Disturb" function. If something was incredibly urgent, then sure, I would pick up my phone in the middle of the night. But realistically that rarely happened. As for emails and other notifications, they just were not important to look over right before bed. I am not a Fortune 500 CEO so it made little sense for me to be glued to my phone.

Next, I made it a habit of getting to sleep at generally the same time each night. This sounds incredibly mundane to do, especially if you are in your early 20's. And let's be honest, this did not happen one hundred percent of the time. That's why the key here is the word generally. If I would go to sleep close to 10-11 PM each night, I felt much more refreshed when I woke up the following morning. If I had the odd night where I was working on a project until 2 AM, my sleep would be disturbed, but it would not have a significant impact on my performance during the day. If I made it a routine to go to bed at whatever time I wanted to, or to wake up at whatever time, I would be teetering so far into chaos and disorder that I would not find any purpose or motivation in the following day for much. This is why I cannot stress enough how much of an impact the habits that you have prior to bed have on the following day.

Be militant in your approach to setting up proper sleep hygiene as well. If you are stressed out or anxious, your quality of sleep will be poor. A simple method to reduce this is to do some night time journaling. It is amazing what introspection can help do for you. Furthermore, reduce the time you spend on what I would deem as extra noise prior to bed. This includes watching tv, scrolling on your phone, or anything else that will stimulate you. And finally figure out what is an appropriate time for you to go to bed and stick to it. When you then wake in the morning, provided that you maintained proper sleep hygiene, you will feel much more refreshed. The next step is to figure out what to do once you wake up. Personally, I suggest you develop a morning ritual that you can follow. This can be as simple as making your bed, making tea or coffee and so forth. Do not be ashamed with your morning ritual. If you need to pray, then pray. If you need to meditate, then meditate. And if you feel that you need to eat a well nourishing breakfast, then I highly recommend that you do that. The bottom line is that you should try to make this morning ritual become a habit that you can stick to and follow through on. What you may soon find is that it is now much easier to get to work on time when you are not stressed or panicking. You may even discover that your mood is elevated or that you are in a much better state of mind to make decisions during the day. That is the power that your morning habits can have on you and the rest of your day.

Chapter 5

The 5 P's

*"He who knows the enemy
and himself will never in a
hundred battles be at risk."*
                    -Sun Tzu

When we aim to accomplish a goal, it rarely ever comes to fruition out of chance alone. Rather, success is dependent on one key factor: preparation. On a day to day basis, we are always in a state where we are preparing for one thing or another. When you make plans to hang out with friends you are spending time and energy preparing beforehand. When you are trying to pass a course in university with an A grade, there is a great deal of preparation that is required. The art of preparation is so ingrained into our DNA that without it we as humans would not be able to survive. It is the fuel that allows us to progress to a desired future. However, there is a stark contrast between planning ahead and completely devoting oneself to meet a specific goal.

There's this quote by Abraham Lincoln where he states that if he had six hours to fell a tree, he would spend the first four hours sharpening his axe. There is a great deal of truth behind that and how preparation works. One of the earliest texts that demonstrated the importance of this type of focused preparation is the *Art of War* by Sun Tzu written in the 6th century BC. Much of Sun Tzu's philosophy on war time preparation is based on the concept of accomplishing a task effortlessly, but it must be done in such a way where there is absolutely zero room for error.

As he describes it in his text: "To rely on rustics and not prepare is the greatest of crimes; to be prepared beforehand for any contingency is the greatest of virtues."

I believe this to be true when it comes to finding the proper balance between chaos and order within our lives. Without proper preparation the goals that we aim for fall apart and push us down into chaos. When we prepare fully, we are in a healthy state of order. If we encounter times of chaos after full preparation, we will not easily be lulled into a state of hopelessness. The reversal is that if we only strive to have complete order within our lives by avoiding any risks or ventures that could put us into a position of chaos, we will not be able to able to reach our highest endeavors. For these reasons, I place a great deal of importance on readying oneself through the mastery of preparation.

"Space I can recover. Time, never"

-Napoleon Bonaparte

Understanding Preparation

Prior preparation prevents poor performance. These were the words that a professor I had in my 4th year at UBC ushered in a lecture hall. The professor of this course was reviewing the scores of our first midterm. Now, the course was not overly difficult, and the test while challenging was not the worst midterm that I had ever written. But overall, the class did not do very well. For a fourth year course our professor definitely had some expectations that he believed the students should have understood by now. This in turn prompted him to bestow upon us the 5 P's. I can recall that a majority of us had done our due diligence when it came to studying for this midterm. In fact, we had prepared for it in the same way we prepared for many of our tests. But the scores did not reflect that. Does this indicate that our methodology for preparation was off? Perhaps. In hindsight, there are always a number of things that could have been done differently. I often reflect on them to be quite transparent. Regardless however, what had happened had already happened. We could now only move on and prepare for the second midterm.

What my professor had said stood out to me more than what many of my other professors had tirelessly ranted about in the courses I had completed. It was like a mantra that made me reevaluate any task that I was attempting to complete. For instance, if I was attempting to meet a goal within a specific amount of time and at a specific place I would repeat this to myself in order to really contemplate what I had to do in order to get to the finish line successfully. It also made me realize that there is a stark difference between what I desired and what I could realistically accomplish. Sure, I could study the day before and stress myself out. I could procrastinate for a long period of time, and finally "prepare." But that is not what preparation is. True preparation, as Sun Tzu articulates, should be carried out with all contingencies in mind. This made me observe what I could rationally accomplish using the resources at my disposal more effectively. Interestingly enough, I found myself less anxious of my own future when I would follow through on daily habits and rituals that engaged me mentally and physically. I found order by writing down my goals and painstakingly adjusting my own life in order to climb the steps required to achieve them.

I believe that another benefit of utilizing preparation in our day to day lives is to minimize procrastination. Often, although we may prepare in great detail by timekeeping, writing down our own schedules or so forth, procrastination is what hinders our ability to plainly complete the tasks that we begin. Why is this? Many psychologists have tried to answer this very question throughout history. Take a psychodynamic approach such as the one proposed by Sigmund Freud. Freud suggests that we procrastinate due to poor behavior stemming from improper toilet training early on in life. I hardly believe that to be the case, and a great deal of psychodynamic psychologists would agree. However, another majority of them happen to believe that the reason that you, and a great deal of other humans on this planet, procrastinate is due to higher neuroticism and self-defeating behavior. Simply, you procrastinate because you have already pre-determined that you will fail. There may be some truth behind this approach. I would suggest however that this approach along with the Arousal Theory of Motivation by Yerkes-Dodson can better help to explain why we procrastinate.

The Arousal Theory of Motivation that was proposed by psychologists Robert Yerkes and John Dillingham Dodson (1908) suggests that performance is optimal when both arousal and stress levels are high enough to influence an increase in mental focus and attention. An example of this is when we may play a sport or write an exam. If our emotions and stress are very high, we may be too rigid to perform. You may have heard of the term "choking" in sports when this happens. The opposite occurs when we are not stressed enough or emotionally incentivized to complete a task. This then leads to underperformance and simply missing the mark. So, perhaps this is the reason that we procrastinate and fall short of meeting the goals that we set for ourselves.

Understand however that there may be a great many reasons for why we do not meet our own expectations at times and inevitably fall short of meeting our goals. But we should not be so discouraged as to create excuses for why we could not accomplish a task that we set out to do. As I have stated numerous times throughout this book, life is unpredictable. We teeter on the chaos and order of our lives tirelessly. And at any given moment we may finally meet the one thing we have been gifted since the moment we are born; death. With that said however, our complex biology and sophisticated evolutionary design has allowed us to thoroughly examine our very existence and the world around us. One of the greatest tools that our ancestors have then used to get us to this very point in time is the ability to prepare for what life has to offer. From the wild environment of East Africa to the modern day concrete jungles we live in, preparation has been the key to our survival.

"To me, it's simple: if you've got the time, use it to get ready. What else could you possibly have to do that's more important? Yes, maybe you'll learn how to do a few things you'll never wind up actually needing to do, but that's a much better problem to have than needing to do something and having no clue where to start."

-Chris Hadfield, *An Astronaut's Guide to Life on Earth*

Keys to Preparation

Taking time out of your day and devoting it to simple tasks such as time keeping, scheduling, and so on is not difficult. If you are in a position currently where things are not going the way you are wanting them to go, then challenge yourself to first define your goals and to come up with a plan of action to meet them. Be thorough with it and be specific. And try to move away from relying on your prior successes and laurels. Just because things worked for you in one setting or situation does not mean that they will work under all conditions. If you go in with that sort of mindset you will soon realize that when you are in a situation where you actually have to prepare, you will find that you cannot do it. And you will fail.

In this game of life make every attempt to have prepared yourself well enough so that you can live a life of true uninterrupted balance. Daily, make it a habit to consider the world and the people around you. Define your goals and pinpoint exactly how you will reach them. And then, simply follow through by doing the work each and every day. You may accomplish a goal in a matter of minutes or days. Some goals may take you longer. But what you will find is that when you have prepared yourself both mentally and physically well enough, miniscule problems will not trouble you. You will be able to react more rationally during times of chaos and function optimally with continued motivation during times of order. Thus, the fulfillment and motivation that you seek out of your life will come from your ability to develop habits based on preparation for yourself that you can carry out each day. Remember, prior preparation prevents poor performance.

Chapter 6

Discipline.

"When nothing seems to help, I go and look at the stonecutter hammering away at his rock, perhaps 100 times without so much as a crack showing in it. Yet at the 101st blow it will split in two, and I know it was not that blow that did it, but all that had gone on before."

-Jacob Riis

Discipline is intriguing to me. In some ways, people believe discipline to be a form of punishment that must be served to get rid of poor behaviors. Or discipline is something that must be carried out on others to achieve a certain outcome. Whatever the case may be, it's hard to argue that discipline is not required in the pursuit of a goal. While contemplating the habits that I believe we should cultivate and develop throughout our life, discipline was at the top of my list. As a matter of fact, much of what we strive to accomplish throughout our lives is very seldom accomplished without an individual taking on accountability and devoting time and resources in the pursuit of meeting a goal. The root of discipline must then come from the individual. Much like our motivations, discipline is the grounding force that drives us to meet our goals and staying true to our path without deviation.

Discipline is so important that it can potentially determine how children will develop into adulthood. A famous study conducted at Stanford University in the late 60's and early 70s highlighted this effect. The Stanford Marshmallow Experiment, led by psychologist Walter Mischel, examined a child's ability to delay gratification. In several studies, children were offered a choice between one small reward that was to be provided immediately or two small rewards if they were able to wait for a short period of time. The tester would then leave the room and return to find that the child had either consumed the marshmallow (or the odd time the treat being a cookie or a pretzel) or had patiently waited, thus allowing them to have double the treat. What researchers discovered following the study was the most important piece to this experiment. It was determined that the children who were able to wait longer for the preferred reward tended to have better life outcomes based on measurements of standardized test scores (SAT), higher attainment in education, and other life measures. Several follow up studies were conducted for more than 30 years with similar results throughout.

To some the take away from the Stanford marshmallow study would suggest that the ability to have self-control and delay gratification is of utmost importance in the development of competent and disciplined individuals from childhood to adulthood. And the evidence is very compelling in supporting this hypothesis. However, there is also an important concept that should be evaluated, and that is the argument of nature versus nurture. To some that are reading this, you may be thinking to yourself that from the beginning you were already at a disadvantage. Perhaps you suffer from attention deficit hyperactive disorder (ADHD), a result of the nature perspective. Or perhaps you were not disciplined at an early age in delaying gratification, which would be an outcome of nurture. Regardless, while there is a significant correlation in the study between delayed gratification at the age of 5 and success in certain life measures by 15, it is not a predictor of success for everyone.

As I discussed in the Mental and Physical sections (refer back to chapters 1 & 2) of this book, we as humans are highly complex and sophisticated organisms. Our brains have developed after millions of years of evolution. And uniquely, our brains continue to develop in different ways over the course of a lifespan. This may be through neurochemical changes and even physical changes through pruning and maturation of synapses. Therefore, much of who we become later in life could be interpreted as two-thirds being based on our experiences and a third being based on genetic predisposition. It is my belief that discipline is the hardest to master because of the need to work against our very biology. Under ideal conditions, we will seek comfort and pleasure when it is available. Much like physical exercise that the body adjusts to over time, it takes time to develop the discipline required to meet a goal.

It is unfortunate how romanticized discipline is. While it is entertaining to watch Sylvester Stallone's training montage in *Rocky* where he is waking up each morning at the crack of dawn, slamming down four raw eggs, running through the streets of Philadelphia and putting in work at his boxing gym, it is not like that for everyone. Life is very mundane. You will experience this firsthand when you move through the various stages of change in order to meet a goal.

There is a reason that we consume this romanticized discipline through pop culture however. Deep down we wish to be like Rocky. We look to fictional characters such as Superman and even celebrities and try to emulate them. It makes sense though, does it not? If they can do it, we can too! This is hardly the case. Through pop culture and media we find the ideal lifestyle that we wish we could have. Anything is better than the mundane life that we currently lead! But what we do not see is the dark side of discipline and what is often required to reach that point.

"Everyone holds his fortune in his own hands, like a sculptor the raw material he will fashion into a figure. But it's the same with that type of artistic activity as with all others: we are merely born with the capability to do it. The skill to mold the material into what we want must be learned and attentively cultivated."

-Johann Wolfgang von Goethe

Transtheoretical Model of Change

To become disciplined enough that we are able to consistently work towards our goals is a difficult process. One of the simplest methods that I can describe to help you achieve this and to develop better discipline skills is by using the transtheoretical model of change. The model, designed by James O. Prochaska, Carlo Di Clemente and colleagues, refers to the temporal model of behavioral change. In simple terms, change occurs through a process of progression through a series of stages. These include precontemplation, contemplation, preparation, action, maintenance, and termination.

When an individual goes through the initial stages and reaches the stages of action, that is when discipline is absolutely crucial to the success of a meeting a goal. This is the stage Rocky gets to when he begins his training montage. Again, you don't really get a chance to see the mundane however that is happening the same time the training montage is happening. If you are embarking on taking action, then you must do it with such strict discipline. Otherwise, you will end up relapsing and heading back to the initial stages. The goal is to become disciplined enough during the action stage that you can move on to the maintenance stage.

At the maintenance stage discipline is absolutely crucial. The case here being that you have now developed the proper skills that allow you to sustain an action for a period of time without preventing relapse. With that said however, an individual is believed to have effectively made a change in their lives when they are able to reach the termination stage. Here, individuals have zero temptation to return back to their old unhealthy habits. Think of it as the moment when Rocky, in *Rocky III,* gets to the point right before the fight when he has finished training. It is at this point that he does not feel lazy or will lose the edge that he had when he was a hungry fighter working his way up.

I felt it necessary to share with you this model and how change can occur in your own life. There is no fool proof program or method to help you achieve your goals, but that does not mean that you cannot do so. It simply relies on you willingness to become disciplined when it matters. That is the difference between the discipline you see that is romanticized and the one based in reality.

Keys To Discipline

So, at its core what needs to be met to encourage discipline? One factor that must be evaluated is the role of the participant. If you, the reader, believe that you need more discipline in your life then you must take responsibility for yourself and ensure that you are militant in fostering habits that encourage such discipline. As a matter of fact, simply being responsible for yourself is a form of discipline. Before you can make any attempt to change the world, you must look to yourself and see how you can save yourself. Are you taking care of your biological needs like clockwork? You are, first and foremost, responsible for yourself and you should make that a priority each day.

A common problem however is that while there may be a need for discipline and a certain degree of willingness to carry out habits that encourage it, the participant forgoes all of this and enters a repeating cycle without going anywhere. And, as I mentioned in the previous chapter, there's a simple word to describe this: procrastination. Procrastination does not discriminate. There are several reasons for why we procrastinate. I believe that instead of fighting procrastination however, we should let it take place. But only momentarily. When we procrastinate we lean on a state of chaos more than order. But procrastination allows us to retroactively observe the reasons for why we may be putting off that task that is important to us. This is, in a sense, a form of exercise where we are encouraging discipline. There is no need to fight fire with fire. Therefore, there must be a process behind minimizing excessive procrastination while taking responsibility. An effective way to do this is to record time that is spent devoted to a goal. Take out a pen and a piece of paper and record what you did over a period of time to meet your goal. Or find some way to record all of your actions. When you do this, you will come to see firsthand how you spend your time daily. It helps keep you accountable and you can find more balance between the states of order and chaos.

Additionally, manage your time well. Time is a luxury that you cannot afford to waste. Schedule your time well in advance. It's much easier to accomplish a task if you know how much time you can devote to it. And if you manage your time well then you immediately enter a period of order rather than dragging along in a period of chaos endlessly. Even if you are late or have missed a scheduled appointment, you will be prepared for it and not overly stressed. It is important to note that failure and discipline go hand in hand. Again, you are not a robot to the point that each and everything in your life must be organized. Be flexible but at the same time be rational. If you can learn from your failures you will encourage more discipline. That is the end goal to all of this. So carefully choose what you do daily when it comes to the tasks that you are looking to complete. Each of your daily habits should encourage some form of discipline.

Chapter 7

The Student, The Master...

"The mind that becomes fixed and stops in one place does not function freely. Similarly, the wheels of a cart go around because they are not held rigidly in place. If they were to stick tight, they would not go around. The mind is also something that does not function if it becomes attached to a single situation."

-Zen Master Takuan Sōhō

There's a story that I'd like to share with you that has been passed down for centuries. In the fifth-century B.C a painting contest was held in Ancient Greece. Here, Zeuxis of Heraclea and his contemporary, Parrhasius of Ephesus (and later Athens) competed against one another to determine the greater artist. Zeuxis was renowned as an innovative Greek painter, known for the realism behind his work. His technique helped him create volumetric illusions by manipulating light and shadow, which was not the norm for its time where artists would fill in shapes with flat colors. Additionally, it is believed that Zeuxis contributed to the composite method of composition and influenced the ideal form of the nude in paintings. A side story recalls how Zeuxis, ever the perfectionist, could not find the appropriate model beautiful enough to pose as Helen. If you are familiar with Greek mythology and have read the *Iliad* and the *Odyssey*, then you will know of the importance behind Helen. She was said to be the daughter of the Greek God Zeus and was known as the most beautiful woman in the world. She was so beautiful in fact, that when she was kidnapped by Prince Paris of Troy, an entire war began between Sparta and Troy. For Zeuxis, a single model would not suffice. So he picked out the finest features on five different models to produce a composite painting of what he determined would be the ideal image of beauty. He was quite the arrogant and proud man you would think.

Now at this contest Zeuxis began to paint his piece of work. The audience that had gathered were surprised when they saw what he had created. On his canvas was a bowl of grapes. Bewildered, the audience could not believe the simple painting that Zeuxis had produced. As they looked on at Zeuxis' painting, a group of birds began to fly down. The birds began to peck at the grapes, much to Zeuxis amusement.

"Look!" he proclaimed. "My grapes are so realistic that not even the birds can tell that it is only a painting!"

He began to boast even more when he looked over at Parrhasius' painting.

"Look at this. He's so ashamed by what he drew that he's hidden his painting behind curtains," he exclaimed.

Parrhasius remained silent as the crowd and Zeuxis erupted in laughter at his painting hiding behind curtains. Zeuxis, now annoyed, walked over to Parrhasius' painting and tried to remove the curtains. And then his expression changed to one of utter disbelief and shock. Try as much as he could, he could not remove the curtains. In fact, the curtains were not curtains at all, but what Parrhasius had painted. Zeuxis looked over at Parrhasius who simply smiled.

"The grapes that you painted may have confused the

birds. But the curtains I painted before you have confused the audience and you", said Parrhasius.

Zeuxis knew he had lost. In this contest Parrhasius had won the battle of realism. He had made Zeuxis look like a fool before an audience. Between the two artists Zeuxis has learned an important lesson that day. No matter how far Zeuxis had come in his art, there was still much for him to learn. He understood at that moment, that although he was so highly praised and looked at himself as a master, he was actually a student. His ego took a hit, but it was a valuable lesson that he learned that day.

At times we are very much like Zeuxis. We put a great deal of focus on what we already know and disregard the importance of continued education or learning. And that's understandable. It is more reassuring to go with the skills that you have already developed rather than learning newer skills. This is especially true if some of those skills are not applicable at the time for the person to learn. There is security in mastering one trade rather than bumbling about having not mastered any at all. However, even then the master must continue to perfect their skills. It is conceited to think that we cannot learn anymore once we have mastered a subject. While there is order and security in mastery, it does not provide true fulfillment and a desire for continued learning and growth. Alternatively, while the life of a student is much more chaotic and undetermined, it does produce more ambition for learning and urgency. The life of both the student and master is tumultuous. But perhaps it is better to not aim to be just a student or master. Rather, it would be better to pursue both. Learn as a student to master a craft and master a subject to further continue your education and refine your skills. When you can do that you will find more fulfillment in your work and achieve a higher purpose.

On a day to day basis you should look to cultivate habits that encourage the pursuit of learning. This is easier said than done, especially if you are not following any formal training or education. I would recommend that you first analyze yourself and determine both your strengths and weaknesses. Perhaps you are excellent at your art or craft but know very little of how to market it or to find a way to live off of it. Or perhaps you have acquired rudimentary knowledge behind a subject and now need to refine the way you must apply it. Take action! The time is now for you to take control of this. And if you are in your twenties or early thirties, you may have the most luxury to use this time wisely.

Whatever you choose to learn, make it a habit of daily practice until you have mastered it. Abandon the fear of failure and dive in head first into learning. Have you ever looked at children and observed the mistakes they make?

A child will fall off of their bike a number of times until they learn how to properly ride it without falling. That is precisely the approach you must have in your life when it comes to learning. And even then when you have mastered something, challenge yourself further. There's a nice little quote by Arnold Schwarzenegger that illustrates this. He states, that if you wish to climb the ladder of success, then you must do so without having your hands in your pockets. While you will teeter on the side of chaos throughout this ordeal, you can rest assured knowing that you have full devotion and control over the direction in which your education is taking you. But do not fall into the trap that you know everything or that you have mastered your craft. The wind blows the hardest at the top of the mountain, or so the saying goes. If you are left unprepared, you will come crashing down to the ground, and often lack the motivation to climb back up. That is utter chaos, and that is not the spot you want to be in.

The true student and the true master

History has revealed to us a number of remarkable human beings that have contributed to modern human history. Great thinkers such as Srinivasa Ramanujan, Mary Shelley, Nikola Tesla, Malcolm X, and so forth. I could write down several great thinkers on pieces of scrap paper and draw them out of a hat to share with you. But there would just be far too many. For the sake of this chapter however, there is one individual that I find absolutely necessary to talk about. And that individual is none other than Leonardo da Vinci. In my humble opinion, Leonardo is the best example of someone who possessed the qualities of a both a student and a master. His work in areas such as architecture, painting, sculpting, mathematics, anatomy, and so forth have lead scholars and historians to deem him a true universal genius. I cannot do Leonardo's works justice in this book alone. That's how much a single human being accomplished in one lifetime. It is mind boggling to consider at times. Many historians determine that the force driving his works was an unquenchable curiosity and fervent imagination. That is also quite remarkable as he can be considered a master in various subjects but did not limit himself to one specialization alone.

"Among his various possible beings each man always finds one which is his genuine and authentic being. The voice which calls him to that authentic being is what we call "vocation." But the majority of men devote themselves to silencing that voice of the vocation and refusing to hear it. The y manage to make a noise within themselves… to distract their own attention in order not to hear it; and they defraud themselves by substituting for their genuine selves a false course of life."

-José Ortega y Gasset

Leonardo was born out of wedlock to the notary Ser Piero da Vinci. Considering the times and the influence of the Roman Catholic Church, your social status within society would ultimately determine how your life would play out. And being born out of wedlock practically branded you for life. Leonardo was barred from studying and practicing any of the professional careers of the time, such as medicine and law. He grew up without a formal education, but remained ever curious of the life around him. His first interest came to drawing what he observed in the countryside in which he grew up in. While other children were being educated, Leonardo would steal paper from the notary his father worked at for his drawings. He paid great attention to detail and overtime his pieces of work attracted his own fathers' attention. Perhaps his father did see something in Leonardo's art, or he saw his chance of finally helping his son progress in life. Either way, his father sent Leonardo to the city of Florence to work as an apprentice under an artist. In Florence he would find himself at the workshop of the great artist Verrocchio.

Verrocchio was the perfect master for Leonardo to learn under. In his workshop Verrocchio encouraged his artists to pay attention to detail like a surgeon and to reproduce what they observed. This was similar to Leonardo's own methods of looking at the fine details of the landscapes in the country side of Vinci and drawing what he saw. And it paid off for Leonardo when he had assisted Verrocchio on his famous painting *The Baptism of Christ*. Scholars and historians alike remark on his very fine brush strokes that were used to paint the angels in the painting. His method would produce an ultra-realistic image that was not too harsh, but not too soft. It is noted that when Verrocchio saw the work Leonardo had produced he was blown away by the gentle quality of the angels faces that seemed to glow on the canvas. Another interpretation of this was that Leonardo had now surpassed the master. But he did not take over Verrocchio's studio. After apprenticing for 6 years, Leonardo set out to make a name for himself.

Leonardo would passionately devote himself to his work for the rest of his life after leaving Verrocchio's studio. He would roam the towns, frequent the brothels and other areas people would congregate at in order to learn and further perfect his art. This unquenchable hunger for knowledge lead him to explore areas such as anatomy and botany. In fact, he would personally dissect and examine cadavers. Soon he would turn towards engineering as evidenced by the elaborate devices that he produced on both paper and life-sized models. At the time of his death, Leonardo was renowned throughout Italy. This is quite remarkable considering that he was given no formal education due to his illegitimacy. To be a true master and a true student yourself, look to Leonardo as an example. In the work that you carry out daily, strive to have a passion for it. Build up the patience to continuously engage in whatever you are doing, even if what you are doing may not always work out as planned. That is the path of the student. And finally, strive to master the art that you are attempting to craft. It would be pointless to attempt learning a skill or art only to abandon it out of boredom. Go as far as possible in your pursuit, and when you feel you have reached the inevitable end of your education, simply let go and transition to something new. Once you have met that you will find the purpose in your work and much more energy and intrinsic motivation behind whatever you do. If you can place an importance on learning as both a master and student, you will open a world of possibility for yourself.

"One can have no smaller or greater mastery than mastery of oneself."

-Leonardo Da Vinci

Chapter 8

Rest and Digest

"True happiness is to enjoy the present, without anxious dependence upon the future, not to amuse ourselves with either hopes or fears but to rest satisfied with what we have, which is sufficient, for he that is so wants nothing. The greatest blessings of mankind are within us and within our reach. A wise man is content with his lot, whatever it may be, without wishing for what he has not."

-Senenca

When I was a child the best time of the year for me personally was when summer vacation would begin. It is quite nostalgic to think about really. On the last day of classes for the school year I would hang out with some of my friends and we would plan on hanging out during the summer vacation. We did not have any phones that we could use to text each other. Back then we would rely on MSN and pretty much figure out what we wanted to do from there. In those two months that we had between the end of classes and before we would start the next grade, I had a great deal of fun. I did not have to worry about the time during the day or worry about going to work. I would spend a lot of time at the local park or biking in the neighborhood. If it was too hot during the day, my siblings and I would sit inside and watch summer tv shows or play video games. My mom would take us to our city's public library where we would pick out all the books we wanted to read over the summer. Couple that with family vacations, although very seldom to ever happen, and visits to our local city pool, summer vacations were the best of times. It was a simple break, and when the following school year would begin, we would be refreshed and ready. I'm sure my parents were also quite happy when their vacation from us would begin.

For the past six years or so my summers have been anything but relaxing. Following graduation from high school I was working a full-time summer job. This was actually the same job I had since the summer following the ninth grade. It was an interesting summer for me as I would spend close to 35-40 hours a week stocking produce in this grocery store. I did not mind it. Sure, I had some more adult responsibilities now. I couldn't spend an entire summer break like a child anymore. But it was not too bad. It flew by quickly and then just like that I was off to UBC. After completing my first year of studies, my summer vacation began a lot earlier than I was used to. I had a full 4 months until I would begin my second year. I worked part time on the side during that summer term while also taking one elective course. I connected with people I had not seen in years in my hometown. And when my second year began at UBC I was refreshed. Looking back on those moments I can now see how much of an impact that rest and relaxation has on performance. When I completed that incredibly rigorous second year of studies I was exhausted. I needed a break. But I was too stubborn to realize this. As my dad likes to say, I have a big ego and I just cannot take no for an answer. I thought I could soldier on and registered for three condensed summer courses with one lab. In doing so it would make my winter term much easier during my third year. Big mistake.

In six weeks I had completed those three summer courses. But it came at a heavy cost. I was mentally exhausted, and I had no idea how to cope with it. There were resources available for students at UBC to help them with the stress that comes from academia, much to their credit, but it just did not help me. When I returned home for the remaining two months of my summer break I was in a very dark place to say the least. I remember that the minute I came back my routine for an entire week was as follows: I would wake up at odd times during the day, much earlier than I wanted to. I would spend all of the day playing video games in my basement. I did not want to associate with anyone. I would not text back or hang out with some of my friends. In the evening, when I was done playing video games, I would go to the gym. Ironically enough, while abandoning all social responsibilities, I still prioritized my health and fitness by watching what I ate and my physical activity. But that was me for a good week or so. Eventually I would get out of this depressive rut and go on to enjoy the rest of the summer, albeit it was probably at about 75% of my regular capacity when compared to the previous year. Think of the glass half full, half empty analogy. My glass was three quarters full. It was not optimal for me, and I walked into my third year with the same chip on my shoulder than I could just go along with whatever and perform really well. But at 75% of my full emotional and mental capacity, and some added mileage of stress to go along with it, it was just not a smart idea.

For the remaining two years of my academic experience at UBC I increased my pace without resting. I worked harder and continued to reap the rewards of all of my hard work. But the end result was worse each time. I was like a drug addict trying to chase that high. The high for me being praise, validity of my efforts, and the eventual undergraduate degree I was pursuing. I did not take off a single academic term of full time courses until the latter half of the summer of 2015. By that time I had just hit a wall of exhaustion. But it was not the same kind of exhaustion I had experienced as before. I was not depressed or anything of the like. Actually, it was the opposite. I just could not stop working. As if my whole life purpose was to just continue doing something. If I was not doing something, or what I deemed productive, I would put myself down greatly. In my pursuit of success and excellence, I continued to neglect my health and wellbeing. Talk about the quickest race to last place. I became more irritable, less agreeable, hot headed, conceited, cynical, narcissistic, and self-defeating.

When I reflect on it now, I realize that I cannot blame anyone but myself for this. I cannot say that it was due to my grandfather's passing that this was happening to me. I cannot say that it was due to the stress of school alone that did it. The onus of what was becoming of me falls on me, and I realize now that I should have taken the personal responsibility to do something about it much sooner so that I could have done something about it. It is also a lot easier said than done however. Imagine drowning in an ocean and asking to throw a life jacket to yourself. For this reason, I place habits that encourage rest and relaxation on my list of what we should pursue each day. For any person that is trying to achieve something or pursue their goals, do not fall into the trap of neglecting your own mental and physical wellbeing. I am saddened by all of the motivational speeches and pseudoscientific new age gurus that encourage simply working hard to achieve a goal. That is hardly the case, and if you do pursue that sort of mindset, I can tell you from firsthand experience that you will not balance the chaos and order in your life. Arnold Schwarzenegger once said, no pain no gain, in reference to how to become a champion in whatever pursuit you have. But even the Austrian Oak knew that there is a difference between outworking others, and defeating yourself in the process. Rest is absolutely important.

The Science behind Rest and Relaxation

There are a number of reasons that rest and relaxation are important in our day to day lives. It can affect our physical wellbeing as well as our mental. Before I get into the finer details of this, I'd like for you to take a minute to understand what rest and relaxation means using the following analogy. Imagine that you have just purchased a brand new vehicle. You have a friend that also purchased the same exact vehicle. Now you've driven this vehicle for some time. This vehicle has hit some bumpy roads along the way but it still works. After a number of years, and added mileage you begin to notice that its performance has decreased. Your friend's vehicle however is running as smoothly as the day it was purchased. How can this be? Perhaps it has not been under the same conditions as your vehicle. Or, perhaps it's the fact that your friend has taken care of their own vehicle. They have regularly had it checked by a competent professional. They have also spent their resources appropriately in order to maintain this vehicle. You on the other hand just have not been very diligent on the upkeep. Your tire blows out while you are trying to get to your destination one day. To fix this problem now you have to pay more out of your pocket. Eventually you encounter more and more problems to the point that it is just not reasonable to continue running with this car any longer. Besides yourself, and maybe some people that have a thrill for dangerous activities, no one else wishes to get involved with the screaming metal death trap that is your vehicle. Do you see where I am going with this? Just like the maintenance of your car, you need to find ways to maintain your own life. And that goes for you, the person living this life! The simplest way to do this is to find ways to relax.

Stress is a common physiological response to a demand or a threat. The issue at hand however is when stress responses occur chronically. Some of the consequences of this is the increased concentration of corticosteroids, such as cortisol in blood. This can further lead to other complications such as increased blood pressure, risk of cardiovascular disease, and shifts in hormone regulation. The effect of stress on the human body can be traced back to the work of researcher Hans Selye (1907-1982). He studied the stress response of lab mice subjected to various physical, antigenic and environmental stressors. Though controversial at the time, his research indicated that the lab mice that were stressed exhibited deterioration of the thymus gland (a specialized lymphatic system organ where T cells mature; involved in immune system function) and an increase in ulcers. Interpretation of Selye's work has led us to now understand the stress response in humans and the role the sympathetic and parasympathetic divisions of our autonomic nervous system have on our body. Many of the stressors that we now face in modern day to day life can be attributed to triggering the onset of our stress responses.

Individuals suffering from chronic stress may exhibit symptoms of increased anxiety, depression, social isolation, abdominal pain including cramping, back pain, and a difficulty to concentrate on a task. Sound familiar? You may be experiencing some of these symptoms when you are stressed over a period of time or know someone who is experiencing this. Some of the finest examples of this is when we lose loved ones or experience some sense of loss or grief. There is no shortage of symptoms that are now being related to increased stress in medicine. The Diagnostic and Statistical Manual of Mental Disorders (DSM-5) states that chronic stress may increase an individual's risk for psychiatric disorders. While I could go into a great deal of detail into stress and its relationship with many health problems, I will refrain from doing so in this book and allow you to explore this more on your own time.

There is an opposite effect that occurs physiologically when we are not stressed. Under this parasympathetic control of our autonomic nervous system our heart rate, ventilation, and hormones are regulated and maintained through a system of homeostasis. Some of the easiest ways to achieve this state is to simply breathe! Although meditation and the techniques around it have surfaced in almost all walks of western life, there is some scientific basis behind it. Studies as far back as the 1980's have demonstrated that deep breathing, or breathing diaphragmatically, dramatically reduces the onset of our fight or flight responses. By practicing this we are able to limit the amount of cortisol that is being secreted and reduce the chance of making poor or rash decisions as a result of increased stress. Additionally, this can also help us cope with emotions such as anger and hostility towards others.

Make no mistake however, breathing and breathing exercises can only help momentarily. While studies have exhibited that breathing and meditation-based exercises can induce activation of our pre-frontal cortex, it should not be treated as the sole prescription for dealing with stress. I am not against medical interventions or the use of pharmaceuticals either to help with bringing us to states of relaxation. But the core concept that I hope that you understand by now is that for all of the high productivity that we wish to have in our lives, we should not disregard the power of rest. To keep your own mental and physical wellbeing in check, make sure to devote a certain part of your day or week to rest-like activities. And if possible, foster habits daily that encourage rest. It may be as simple as taking five minutes out of your day to focus on your breathing and even as complicated as retreating to a place of comfort momentarily. Whatever it may be, be sure to rest and digest.

"We are living in a culture entirely hypnotized by the illusion of time, in which the so-called present moment is felt as nothing but an infinitesimal hairline between an all-powerfully causative past and an absorbingly important future. We have no present. Our consciousness is almost completely preoccupied with memory and expectation. We do not realize that there never was, is, nor will be any other experience than present experience. We are therefore out of touch with reality. We confuse the world as talked about, described, and measured with the world which actually is. We are sick with a fascination for the useful tools of names and numbers, of symbols, signs, conceptions and ideas."

-Alan Watts

Chapter 9

Gratitude

"Remember to conduct yourself in life as if at a banquet. As something being passed around comes to you, reach out your hand and take a moderate helping. Does it pass you by? Don't stop it. It hasn't yet come? Don't burn in desire for it, but wait until it arrives in front of you. Act this way with children, a spouse, toward position, with wealth—one day it will make you worthy of a banquet with the gods"

-Epictetus

How do you start your day? And how do you end it? Are you truly thankful for what you have, or do you shake your fist to the sky cursing God or whatever force for the cards that you have been dealt? This is the final topic that I will share with you in this book; the alluring power behind cultivating habits of gratitude. You see, I am incredibly fortunate and privileged to reside in a country where universal health care is available. I could go bankrupt tomorrow, and possibly even be forced to live on the streets. And yet this outcome would not even remotely come close to resembling the many that sleep on the sides of roads in cities like New Delhi or even Cape Town. At least here if I was homeless and hungry I could turn to a number of options. I could go to the local Sikh Gurdwara (temple) and eat food provided by the volunteers. I could go to a shelter. I could even commit a crime, go to jail, and still have a life of luxury in a sense. Yes, when I think about it, I am truly very fortunate.

I find that when I talk to others, especially young people that are attending classes at a university, there is often an absence of gratitude in their speech. I'm sure you've probably encountered these types of people in your day to day lives. The woman who may complain that the milk used in her latte from Starbucks was not organic. The man that may incessantly complain about how his fast food took five minutes to be prepared. Or even the child that wails at the top of his lungs in a supermarket when his mother, overly exhausted and who has perhaps even checked out at this point, will not purchase a new toy for him. We've all come across these people. Some of us are these people! But we quietly brush it aside.

"That's not my problem," is what the spectator says out loud in their head.

"This is the absolute worst!" is what those that are in these predicaments may think.

These are actual first world problems, joke or not. Now, that's not to suggest that only those who grew up with a privileged lifestyle are like this. I have met just as many ungrateful people from all other walks of life. At their core they are really all the same. They are bitter with what life has given them. They resent their friends, families, and colleagues that may be doing much better than them economically and financially. They blame others for their constant misfortunes. These people are truly stuck in a cycle of never-ending chaos. What is most unfortunate is that they can escape this hell anytime they wish. This is not a secret. There is no great power outside of the self either that will help them escape their self-imposed exile through misery and misfortune. They hold the power to resolve their own problems and shift between chaos and order. Only, they choose not to. It's much easier to complain than to take action. And one of the easiest methods to escape this spiraling hell is to simply be grateful.

I once had a psychology professor during my under-graduate years at UBC that some referred to as the happi-ness professor. Dr. Mark Holder, an Associate Professor at the University of British Columbia Okanagan (at the time of this writing), researches the science of happiness. I found this to be quite interesting. While most psychology researchers were looking at everything that makes us un-happy, from neurochemistry and social psychology, there were very few that looked at happiness itself based on so-cial relations and spirituality. I can distinctly remember one lecture I had where Dr. Holder was describing his research and sharing with us how gratitude can have a positive effect on our lives. First he described to us how there were eighteen different definitions for depression in the *Dictionary of Psychology* while there were exactly zero for happiness. That was quite alarming to hear. He then asked the students in the lecture hall to participate in a simple activity.

"Pull out a scrap piece of paper and write down six things that you are grateful for in your lives. Make it unique. Make it personal," he said.

I obliged, and I wrote down the six things I was grateful for. And voila, nothing happened. I did not feel any happier. My life did not change. But that was not the purpose behind this exercise. What Dr. Holder was conveying through the exercise was to observe the things in our lives that bring us a bit of positivity. There was uniqueness to actually writing out what I was grateful for rather than contemplating things that I am thankful for. Looking at my list I could see what filled me up emotionally and mentally so to speak. I could see the social relationships that were a positive impact in my life. I could see, out of just six things that I wrote, how much I really had. Now that made me happy. I began to make it a habit of nightly writing down five to ten things I was thankful for during the day. Once a week, I would sit with a coffee in one hand, and jot down on a piece of paper the things I valued in my life. This weekly list would change at times based on priorities of course, but it kept me firmly rooted and appreciative of what I had. I felt happier. But it did not just bring happiness into my life. It brought order.

Gratitude, especially in times of chaos can help to bring order. The reverse of this is that it can also help us observe the self during times of order and what chaos will need to look like in order to meet a goal. As stated throughout this book, both chaos and order are necessary for balance to occur in our lives. If order and chaos are each a scale on opposite ends, then gratitude is one of the central foundations that holds up that scale. With regards to happiness, it should not solely be the goal that is pursued through gratitude. That is only scratching the surface. Watch your day to day habits and observe if they bring you to a place of profound gratitude rather than simple happiness. Alternatively, as current scientific research shows, certain habits we carry out each day can bring us a wealth of happiness. This includes nurturing social relationships as I mentioned earlier, being accountable for yourself, and finding what you are passionate about. Use that to your advantage when you are trying to organize your life. I believe that last point to be very important too. Why do you do what you do on a day to day basis? If you sit around on the couch all day playing video games and watching tv, just what are you aiming for? You will hardly be grateful for that, and if you are it is only momentary and fleeting. No, rather it will do you better to look beyond short-term self-indulgences.

My recommendation for leading a fulfilled life is to listen to the self and to find purpose in what you do daily. The intrinsic gratitude you bring forth daily is what will help you overcome a goal. It is infectious and will affect those around you. People will gravitate towards you, not because you are some saint, but because of your openness. It is natural to be attracted to things that do not cause us harm. That is the energy you attract. That is power. Do not mistake this for fleeting positivity or pseudoscience behind speaking what you want or have into existence. When you can set aside all of the noise and pinpoint what you have and what you are striving for, you begin to balance your life. No longer are you teetering between moments of chaos and order. You have full control and can barter for your future more effectively. That is a better deal than roaming aimlessly throughout life, bitter and resentful, if you ask me.

Additionally, disregard or abandon habits that bring you down based on who you are as the individual. Choose what and who you compare yourself and your life to. If you are comparing yourself to others and what they have, stop immediately. Just because your neighbor purchased a brand-new vehicle does not mean that you must as well. All that you are doing is fueling your own conceit and ego. And when you do that, you fall from being true to yourself and what you can become. Instead, focus on what you can do today to meet the true version of yourself. Appreciate the people you encounter in your day, regardless of their attitudes towards you. Whether it was a good moment or a bad moment, there is a glimpse of reality behind it and you can learn a great deal from it. Finally, write it all down. Keep a record of what you are grateful for. And continue to encourage that daily. Soon you will see that the path ahead of you is heaven compared to hell. It will become easier to savor small moments when you are not worried about factors outside of your control. It will become easier to forgive and let go of animosities towards others while maintaining your own self-respect. All of this, your physical and mental health, your purpose in life, and what you accomplish with your time on this planet will all fall place. So be grateful because it costs you next to nothing, yet the rewards are bountiful.

Acknowledgements

As I stated at the beginning of this book, this has taken me 25 years to write. But I could not have written it without certain people and events that took place in my own personal life. I first would like to thank my mother and father for bringing me into this world at 2:53 pm on January 14, 1993. They nurtured and raised me to become the man that I am today. Along with that, I would like to thank both my brother and sister for supporting me while also arguing with me over the years. I would like to thank my grandfather who always supported me, regardless of the circumstances. It hurts me to this day that he could not have seen me accomplish many of the goals I had set out to accomplish. But I cherish the 22 years of love and discipline he instilled in me. It has taken me some time, but I know now he was always proud of me regardless of my accomplishments. Along with him, I thank my grandmother for always looking out for me. As my cousins can recall, she was a very stern but loving woman. Unfortunately, she developed Alzheimer's Disease while I was young... Still, I thank her for being a part of my early life and looking out for me. I also thank my grandfather and grandmother on my mother's side for giving me love and affection when I was younger. I would further like to extend a thank you to all of my relatives on both my mother and father's side that have played some part in my life. I am thankful for all of my friends and acquaintances, past or present, for having a part to play in my development. I am thankful for the teachers, coaches, and mentors that I have studied under and learned from. I am grateful for both the University of British Columbia and the University of the Fraser Valley where I have studied...

I wrote this book while listening to Nas' *Illmatic* album. At times I would find myself hitting a writer's block or so and this album provided me with the creativity to continue writing. Many of the chapters I wrote were written in a single sitting while listening to Jay-Z's early albums (*Reasonable Doubt, The Black Album, In My Lifetime Vol 1.,* etc) along with some music by Nujabes. I also found comfort in lo-fi hip hop music that I came across on YouTube. It is amazing how moving music can be at times...

I am also thankful for the many different books that I have read in the 25 years I have been on this Earth. A great deal of influence has come from graphic novels and comic books that I have read over the course of these years. First, I'd like to thank Stan Sakai for creating *Usagi*

Yojimbo. There is something special behind the childish humor in his comic book series. I was also inspired by the works of Takehiko Inoue, especially from his series *Vagabond.* A lot of my creativity at an early age came from the works of Akira Toriyama, notably his *DragonBall* series. I always wished I could go Super Saiyan! Many of these works really opened the door for me to explore the world outside of the town that I lived in for most of my life and I owe them a great deal of thanks...

As I have mentioned in this book already, Viktor Frankl's *Man's Search for Meaning* gave me a base for rationalizing some of my own thoughts. I would also add Marcus Aurelius' *Meditations* and Miyamoto Musashi's *Book of 5 Rings* to the list of books that have inspired me. I often return to reading *Animal Farm* by George Orwell as well at times for a very sobering history lesson...

Finally, I would like to thank you, the reader, for supporting me by purchasing this book. I thank you for considering my work. My hope is that the words I have written here may spark a discussion or simply provide comfort for those going through a difficult period in their own lives. Remember, you are the captain of your own ship as you navigate it through the waters of life. I hope that you may reach the destination that you have set course for.

Yours truly,

Sandeep Poonian

www.ingramcontent.com/pod-product-compliance
Lightning Source LLC
Chambersburg PA
CBHW021133020426
42331CB00005B/752